# A Love Unborn

Lulu Redden

BookLeaf Publishing

India | USA | UK

Presentation by *BookLeaf Publishing*

Web: www.bookleafpub.com

E-mail: info@bookleafpub.com

ISBN: 9789360941062

First edition 2024

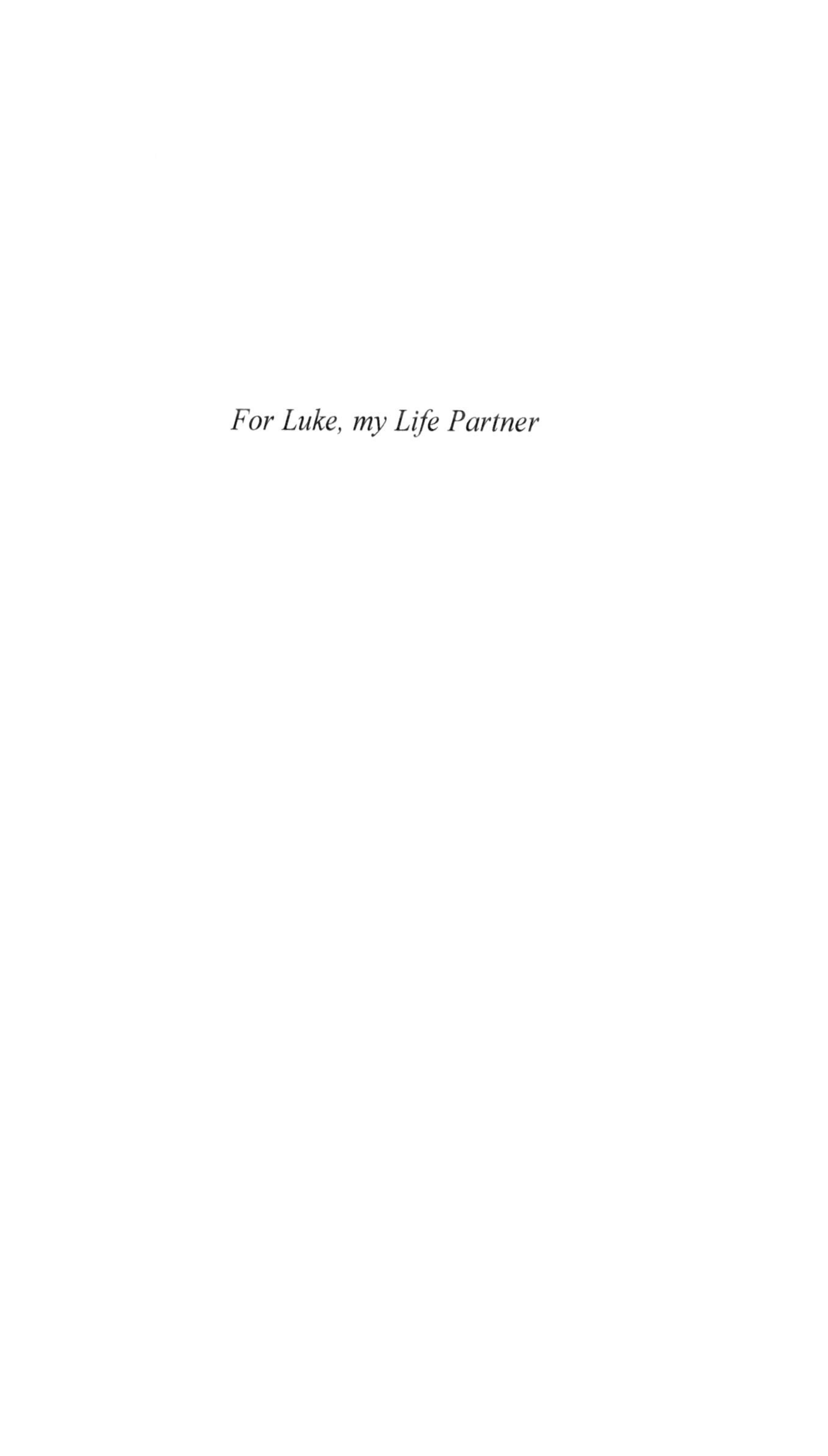

*For Luke, my Life Partner*

# Maya

Maya told me I was
But a ripple in a smooth lake.

She was skipping stones and said,
"We're all ripples and then we pass."

# Softly, we all fall down

Manic moods rise
    and fall with the moon
  mounting the ocean's tide
      ascending the mortal bride.
Lunacy:
    High is divine conception
                beneath the
cresting surf;
         low is bone dry pearls
disintegrating into dust.
           High is the
beaded heads of water
  upon a bed of clover;
low is the rotating blades
of his lawn mower.

             High is

the chit chit chatter

our quick wit frothing forth;
          low is an empty
coffee cup
 the stained ceramic, cracked.
High is a birth,
        our bright angel's reception;
low is the cacophony of wails

from the lingering ghosts
of unwanted children.
                    Melancholy:
Disordered bodies ride
    a roller-coaster of ego;
then softly,
      we all fall
down.

# Irregular Poo Haikus

Brown

A typical turd
From a regular movement
Firm round cylinder

Yellow

Almost pure liquid
Rapid diarrhea squirts
IBS worsens

Green

Quick kale moves through me
A salad tossed too quickly
Burning bowels pass green

Purple

Licorice drip drop
Won't stop: purple explosions
Love me some anis

Red

Open wide rectum
Crimson tide is now coming
A wound in your gut

IBS

Constipation's hard
My Irritable Bowel Syndrome
Squirts diarrhea

# My Thesis Bride

Walking, I am surrounded by fall:
The crunch of a leaf, the rain of acorns, and you,
My Dear Thesis.

We chat in the coffee shop:
You recommend yet
"Another angle."

I watch you on YouTube:
You burn bright brilliant profanity
out of the mouth of comedians.

I court you,
Try to seduce you
Too.

One sweet night,
On my favorite couch at the UNC Charlotte
library,
You mutter out of my screen:

"Member"
"Grandma's fucking shit"
A Comedienne's fat pussy.

Now, I simply cannot get
Margaret Cho's siren song, "My Puss"
Out of my head.

But mostly,
My Dear Thesis,
I can't find You:

My Tool
To Deconstruct
This Madness.

Winter edges it's elbows in and reminds me:
Yet another graduate student boat
Will set sail without me.

I'll have to wait another semester
For my Pregnant Fiancée
And all of her brassy betrothal luggage.

Dear, I fear
I cannot carry you another season.
The midnight library is far too lonely.

But we've already signed a contract,
And I've already paid my fees,
And for what?

For you to just sit there

In complete
Silence!?!

Oh, HELL no- you're coming with me-
Even if I have to drag your ass
Through the racial muck and back…

I am about to
Lose my
Patience!

My Dear Bride,
I know you were only made of paper,
And I am so sorry.

Your busted lip will heal,
And they will soften your scars
With a salve.

If my family pays for another term
At the Academe
They will offer me:

A handful of tissues to keep me from weeping
too loud.
And Pilar to keep me going, and going, and
going
Like the Energizer Bunny.

I've committed myself to you, Dear Thesis.
I am never going to leave you
Unless you say, "we're through" or "I do" to
another scholar.

Humor is a bitch to write about.
I can't say my Pilar didn't warn me
That Pragmatics and Humor were tricky.

Mix in Race,
And you've go yourself
A sharp knife.

My dangerous beautiful Fiancée,
I will lasso you in a golden ring,
To protect you from the Editor.

But, no, I WILL NOT sign
A prenuptial agreement.
Don't be so greedy!

Marriage is for Life,
So tame your lashing tongue
And I will feed you structure.

"I do."
"I do."
(Kiss)(Kiss)(Sign)

Mrs. Laura Redden Erturk and Mrs. The
Construction of Race and Identity in the
American Stand-Up Comedy of Margaret Cho
and George Lopez
Married May 2014 at the University of North
Carolina Charlotte
Officiated by Pilar Garcés-Conejos Blitvich,
Elizabeth Miller, and Rebecca Roeder

# Dear Universe

You were always there.
We always knew,
But we resisted with fear.
We continue to resist You,
Yet we love through Your love.
Why judge the Universe
When Your silent voice
Roars through still waters?

# The Other Woman

I am the Other Woman

My power over men is nothing.
As a black hole vacuum, I suck in.
As seductress, I am the one in his head
While she is the one in his bed.

She is the reality, the dependable wife,
The preferred Life Partner.
I am the dream and the potential.
The Ultimate Question

I am...
Alone in a land of possibility.
We see each other while asleep.
You are an individual man with a woman,
and I could possibly be any other woman.

Single, we may be available.
You want us because we
Have the power to just be,
While she intends to do and undo you,
Weaving her soul into hers.
She sews;
We are.

This is why sometimes
When she does you one too many times,
You offer to buy me a drink,
And then you ask me to undo you
In order to pull you
Into the great nothing
That I am.

Your heart is a marionette;
She works the strings and weaves.
You leave me alone,
But still I silently yearn.
When my desire inhales,
You are left empty.
Freedom
I am.

"Nice to met you, my name is Desiree,"
Your wife's eyes
Grow greener in this light,
While mine are unrealized red.
She'd like to end me where I exist,
but I am guiltless,
The Other Woman
I am.

# Fridge Poetry for Tall Mountain Sun

A.      Do you believe in sugar
        And feel
         a brail goddess?


B.      Just You

        Before an airport
        You must taste one word:
        Me.

        You would make it
        Out of here happy
        Because you'd be set.

        You'd be wearing
        Astronaut pants and a name tag...
        Die happy.


C.      Can I marry a floor?

            Hey!
                I'm your sign somewhere
                    Out of this world.

Didn't I see
      Love at first sight
          Or is it against me?

I'm wrong:
      I thought that was
          As good as gold.

I'm sorry:
      Walk by again
          Tequila.

# Shutting off a burning spigot

INSOMNIA:
Heavy eyes.
Nodding off
In
The
Sho
Wer.

Burning candle:
Gaudy glittering stars.
Lick
And Press.
Siz
Zle.

Breasts too high:
Gurdle-thin strangulation.
Suck
And Faint
Ovar
Ies…

On Fire:
New moon ritual burns.
Burn

And Bring
Ba
Bies.

Rain that patters:
Rhythm induces sleep.
Inhale.
Hold.
Exhale.
Shut off.
s
  l
    e
      e
        p.

# Poo Haikus Written on Porcelain Pots

Gentle was the fart
But that did not much matter
The poo went splatter

The porcelain chair
Is where I grunt in despair.
Now I need fresh air

Float along brownie
In the depths of toiletry.
Be wasted, my friend.

# Una Declaración de los Derechos de la Mujer

He stood in the doorway nude like a statement,
Bold like an answer or the end.

I was the means to an end
The procreator of questions.

His eyes held hints of delight, and almost
wonder.
Flecks of inquiry sparkles in his irises.

Still, they stated the emotion,
Instead of asking me mine.

My emotion is a question mark in motion,
A curve that continues infinitely,

As a declaration of women's rights.

# Existence is an empty night

Have you heard the electrical impulses,
Charging zippity plop throughout your brain,
Like the crackling old television static?

I wish humans had knobs. I would turn them on.
I would keep my television set unbearably loud
To keep my many voices muted.

But I'm trapped in this vacuum on pause.
From the box, I pound at the glass from the
inside.
You watch me blank faced and unamused.

I'm just a dot among the salt and pepper fuzz.
Just a single static pop
Crackling in all that buzz.

Throw a brick! Bust me out!
Or at least change the channel,
So I can sneak out on the edge of a sound wave
cloud.

I slip, and radiate
From the chaos towards infinity.
I cease to exist.

Empty on the outside
Where sound and light have vanished,
I am swallowed by Our Great Dark Knight.

# Collaborative Fridge Poetry
# with My Love

Drive faster
Sing about bitter chocolate
And smell women.

"As gorgeous goddess
I want less butt hair."

Spray my urge
But stop their suits of army-
Fashion headed by bare black feet.

At pant recall
These Ofatofan

# Pearly Poo Haiku

Blue

Strange slippery shit
Like toothpaste: Could be a Smurf
Drinking blue Kool Aid

Rainbow

Poo of every hue
A unicorn has been here
Collect a sample!

Pearl

Inside pearly poo
Iridescent shades sparkle
With my love unborn

# Inertia

You don't want to move.
You stay home and binge watch Netflix
On a sad sagging couch crater,
Swallowing your motivation.
You bundled up with a few furry friends,
And don't move for days on end.
Inert.

Though Depression has incapacitated you,
Life and roommates continue moving,
Compelling you to relocate once again:
Boxes, crates, books, mates,
A rotation of things and people.

Yet you sit there imagining you have a choice of
not moving.
Inertia is inevitable death,
So you start moving,
And you will continue to move
Until the end.

# The Community Orchard

Here at the Mulberry tree, we meet, greet, plan
and circulate our motions.
This is the communal center and the beating
heart of Rosewood Orchard.

We came together today to discuss our compost
heap at the edge of our property,
Where we have buried our orange peels, apple
peels, and egg shells.

When I worked at Starbucks, I used to bring
heavy sagging bags of
Used coffee grounds to fertilize, aerate and
acidify our pile of dirt.

At Halloween, a skeleton pops its head up out of
our compost.
We are reminded of death and the life that it
brings.

A sustainable soil that nurtures the grounds from
which we feed.
Dead matter decomposes and produces new
growth.

Our compost pile is not just a place to bury our
waste,
But also a source of nutrition and fertility.

While we meet at the beating Mulberry heart
center,
To discuss our orchard's gut: its compost pile.

We care for all parts of this Community body:
An herb spiral, a frog pond, numerous crab
apple trees, trellises…

Our beloved compost heap helps us circulate our
nutrients,
And we must build a more solid structure to
contain and spread our Energy.

# Egg Yolk Sun

If I don't write, a little piece of me dies.
Crack open my head, and release
The runny yolk of my being.

Time flies and I let the Universe drive
Into that egg yolk sun
While my thoughts come undone.

# Earth Sky and Water*

Whether studying snails
Or riding red horses,
Flying V-formations
Or shooting super-stars
We experience our world daily.

The sea flows into night,
As Earth consumes the light.
We celebrate daylight,
Then dusk, darkness, twilight.

Fish twist and slither to frogs,
Emerging from tadpole-tails.
Pelicans consume them all,
Then take flight into seagulls.

Verbum is the spotted white
Scattered through the soil and sky.
The sun dusts our body off,
Then disappears into night;
All sensation sleeps until morning.

*inspired by MC Escher's "Verbum"

# Our First Swallow

"Let's have a mindful beer, together," said
A—and so we did.
The glass was cold, solid on delicate fingertips.
Our glasses clinked; we closed our eyes, and
took our first swallow.
Our friend was the beer, so we gave it our firm,
undivided attention.
We listened and watched with eyes gently
closed.
Who are you, beer?

There was no label, no known source.
All was in the taste, look, and sound: the full
experience.
Caramel exploded on our tongues deep within
the crevices of our mouths,
As beer swam between our pearly whites.
It frothed, fizzled, cracked, and crystalized at the
places that we met.
Beer stayed with us as it rolled down our
tongues,
Slithering its fingers along our throats.
It reached the place between our lungs and all
sensation ceased
As B—absorbs into us?

That was our first swallow.
Our eyes opened.
A—smiled, "it's nice!"
Our eyes closed.
Where is B—?

We looked for that which had disappeared.
We rushed down deep into our guts,
but we could not feel where the dragons lay
dormant.
We crawled back up into our brains and looked
at them straight in the eye:
B—wasn't there.

So, we waited and watched clouds drift, like a
sheep counting sheep.
Thoughts ambulated as pedestrians on a city's
conveyer belt.
B—might be attached to one of them.

But then we realized beer was a thought, so
poof!
Again it disappeared.
Watching, waiting, trying to listen.
I'm never going to find B—

Wait. Watch. Listen.

Entities strolled by: each, a snowflake; each,
infinitely amusing.
A leering stranger appeared:
eyes rolling back, it's mouth foaming,
but the unknown passes on by like all the others.
As it's shadow fades, we sighed relief,
stifling clinging, hesitant judgments—
Then, it turns around to face us—
Before we can inquire about the whereabouts of
our Friendly Foe, it vanishes.
Hey, wait—was that B—?

The thought was just a thought;
the stranger, just an image;
the fear, just a sensation.
We label each one by one as they disappear.
Ommm. Oooommmmm. Oooommmmmmm.
Oooooooo—ah—mmmmm—ah—

A Buzz, a Vibration, the Energy pulsating, the
Synapses throbbing:
The Energy that is B—within me—
Is B—here?

No, it was just my cell on silent, vibrating
through my left jeans pocket.
I tried my best to ignore it; it desired to be
because I resisted it.
But it kept on and on and on and on…

My hand dove towards my pocket, as the pulsing
ceased:
Who's calling me, damn it?

Silence.  Then, the clinking of glasses at the bar,
As other chit chit chattering beings coexisted
with mindful me.
I opened my eyes.
Beer is here in front of us:
A bubbling beverage to be consumed—not
friend nor foe;
Just liquid in a glass sitting right here, right now.
B—is here.

A—looks at me, winks and asks, "Cheers
again?"
We toast and take our second swallow.
B—here now.

# Virginia Beach

This evening, seagulls spread
Themselves over the wake.
Artificial beach lights
Bounced off their bodies.
From afar, they appeared as
Glowing plankton: luminescence
Sparkling on and off,
Moving down and up,
Abreast the crests of waves.

I almost crested.

But a beach comber
With a metal detector
Distracted my ascent.

# A Love Unborn

In winter you landed me.
I walked week by week
Trembling with sand in my undergarments,
Grating, almost satisfying, yet...
Never enough to create a pearl.

I needed the sea to wash over me.
You did not desire my clam shell soul,
And instead of pearls, jades formed
In my mush-innard squish of dry emotion.

You wetted the coral reef,
And danced among her skeletal cavities.
On the shore alone, I opened my shell a moment
Hoping for the moisture of your tongue,
But as I dried and solidified,
I closed once again.

You said we'd never be together.

Now the coral reef has disappeared,
Hands outreached, a mirage, a warm sunny first
love
That would never end
Until you awoke.

It's over now and I'm sure,
Since you looked into the brightness of her
being
So long and so hard,
That you still see her framework
Outlined in purple beneath your eyelids.

But what of that little clam shell you caressed
In such a way that let in grains of sand?
What do you see with your eyelids open and
aware
Of a once welcoming solid shoreline?

# Draconian Unicorn

Red dragons are carnivores,
Blow fire, eat flesh and seek heat.

Purple dragons are omnivores,
Shoot lightning, eat life, and seek nourishment.

Blue dragons are neither,
Expel ice, eat air, seek isolation.

After searching for a unicorn for almost a year,
I finally looked in the mirror:

Unicorns exist!

I ought not seek at all,
As I am already here.

Unicorns are rainbows,
Radiate love, and eat only truth.

Draconian in blood, unicorn in essence,
I may change form and method of consumption,

But I seek only myself.
I cannot be summoned, only sought.

I exist and can also disappear.
I cannot be consumed by fire, lightning, or ice,

Nor can I be captured by desire
Weaving a mask of love.